SIMONE
BILES

BY REBECCA SABELKO

TORQUE™

BELLWETHER MEDIA·MINNEAPOLIS, MN

Torque brims with excitement perfect for thrill-seekers of all kinds. Discover daring survival skills, explore uncharted worlds, and marvel at mighty engines and extreme sports. In *Torque* books, anything can happen. Are you ready?

This edition first published in 2023 by Bellwether Media, Inc.

No part of this publication may be reproduced in whole or in part without written permission of the publisher. For information regarding permission, write to Bellwether Media, Inc., Attention: Permissions Department, 6012 Blue Circle Drive, Minnetonka, MN 55343.

Library of Congress Cataloging-in-Publication Data

Names: Sabelko, Rebecca, author.
Title: Simone Biles / by Rebecca Sabelko.
Description: Minneapolis, MN : Bellwether Media, 2023. | Series: Torque. Sports superstars | Includes bibliographical references and index. | Audience: Ages 7-12 | Audience: Grades 4-6 | Summary: "Engaging images accompany information about Simone Biles. The combination of high-interest subject matter and light text is intended for students in grades 3 through 7"– Provided by publisher.
Identifiers: LCCN 2022050071 (print) | LCCN 2022050072 (ebook) | ISBN 9798886871623 (library binding) | ISBN 9798886872880 (ebook)
Subjects: LCSH: Biles, Simone, 1997–Juvenile literature. | Women gymnasts–United States–Biography–Juvenile literature.
Classification: LCC GV460.2.B55 S24 2023 (print) | LCC GV460.2.B55 (ebook) | DDC 796.44092 [B]–dc23/eng/20221019
LC record available at https://lccn.loc.gov/2022050071
LC ebook record available at https://lccn.loc.gov/2022050072

Editor: Kieran Downs   Designer: Gabriel Hilger

Printed in the United States of America, North Mankato, MN.

TABLE OF
CONTENTS

WINNING GOLD! 4
WHO IS SIMONE BILES? 6
BECOMING A GYMNAST 8
A SUPERSTAR! 12
BILES'S FUTURE 20
GLOSSARY 22
TO LEARN MORE 23
INDEX 24

WINNING GOLD!

Simone Biles takes the floor. The music starts. She moves to the sound.

Biles steps back into a corner. She races across the floor. She flips and twists high in the air. She lands the Biles! Her famous move is one of the most difficult in **gymnastics**. Biles wins her fourth gold medal at the 2016 Rio **Olympic Games**!

5

WHO IS SIMONE BILES?

Simone Biles is an American artistic gymnast. Many people believe she is one of the greatest gymnasts to ever **compete**!

SIMONE BILES

BIRTHDAY	March 14, 1997
HOMETOWN	Spring, Texas
EVENTS	vault, uneven bars, balance beam, and floor exercise
HEIGHT	4 feet 8 inches
JOINED	U.S. Junior National Team in 2012

Biles has more medals than any other American gymnast. She has won 32 medals at World **Championships**. She has also earned 7 Olympic medals. She is the first American woman gymnast to win 4 gold medals at a single Games!

7

BECOMING A GYMNAST

Biles grew up in Spring, Texas. When she and her sister were very young, they were adopted by their grandparents. They became the girls' parents.

BILES'S PARENTS

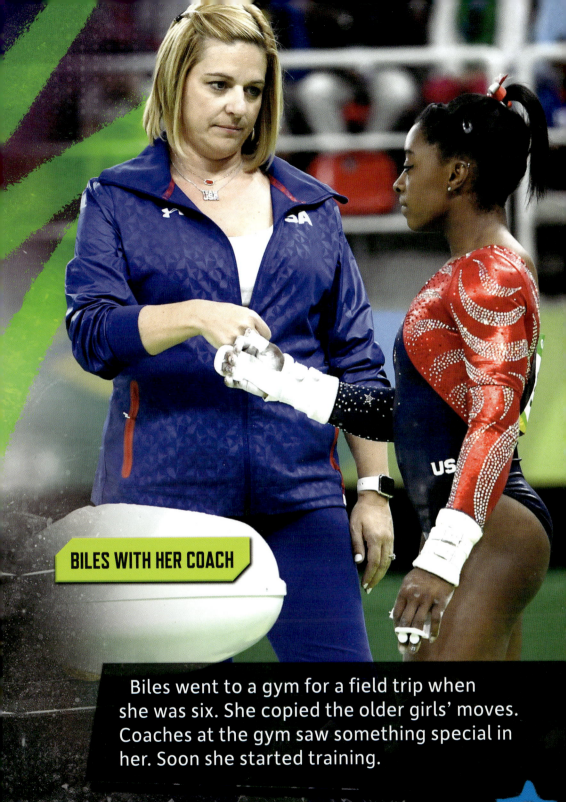

Biles went to a gym for a field trip when she was six. She copied the older girls' moves. Coaches at the gym saw something special in her. Soon she started training.

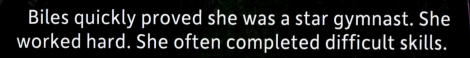

Biles quickly proved she was a star gymnast. She worked hard. She often completed difficult skills.

Biles won a gold medal in **floor exercise** at the 2010 **Junior** Olympic National Championships. She also earned a bronze medal in **vault**. Biles continued to win medals over the next two years. She earned a spot on the U.S. Junior National Team!

2012 SECRET U.S. CLASSIC – JUNIOR LEVEL

10

SPIET

FAVORITES

COLORS

purple
and yellow

SNACK

s'mores
cookies

BOOKS

The Hunger
Games series

**SCHOOL
SUBJECT**

history

11

A SUPERSTAR!

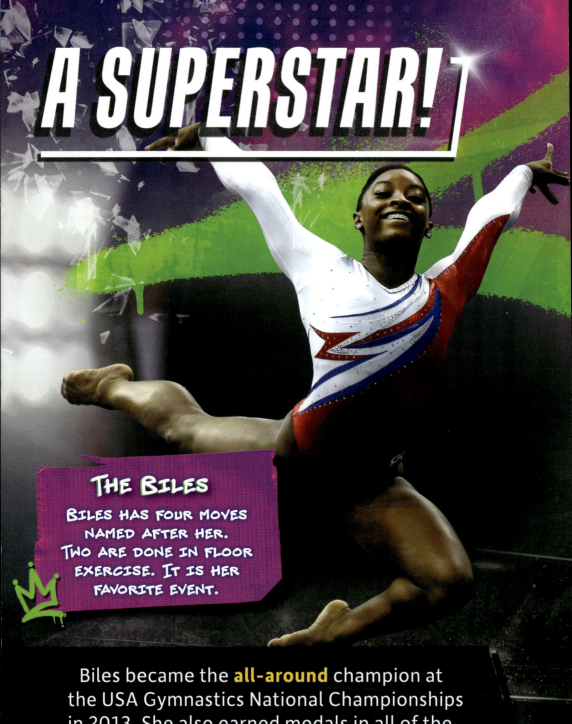

THE BILES

BILES HAS FOUR MOVES NAMED AFTER HER. TWO ARE DONE IN FLOOR EXERCISE. IT IS HER FAVORITE EVENT.

Biles became the **all-around** champion at the USA Gymnastics National Championships in 2013. She also earned medals in all of the individual events.

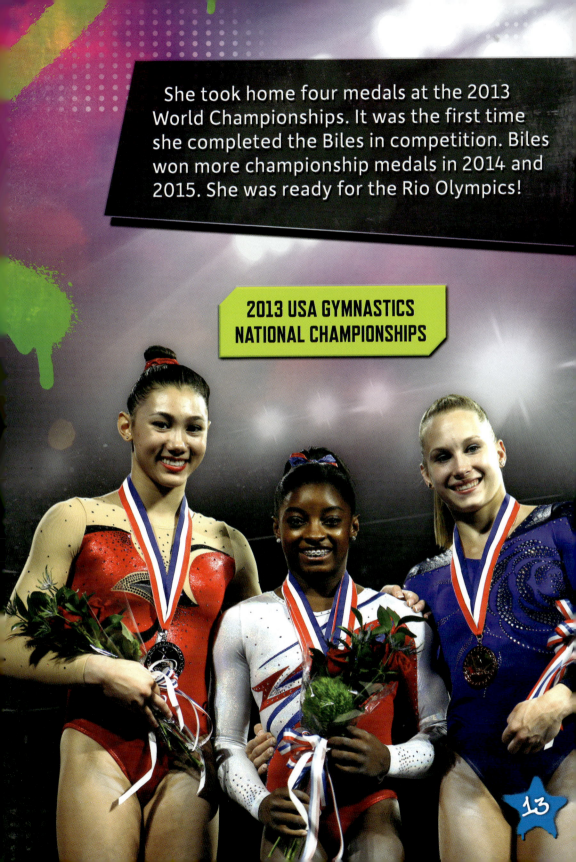

She took home four medals at the 2013 World Championships. It was the first time she completed the Biles in competition. Biles won more championship medals in 2014 and 2015. She was ready for the Rio Olympics!

2013 USA GYMNASTICS NATIONAL CHAMPIONSHIPS

BILES ON BALANCE BEAM

Biles arrived at the 2016 Rio Olympics ready to win! She led Team USA to gold in the team event.

Biles won individual gold medals in vault and floor exercise. She also earned a bronze medal in **balance beam**. She showed the world and herself that she was the best!

14

SIMONE BILES MAP

○ 2016 Rio Olympic Games, Rio de Janeiro, Brazil
○ 2020 Tokyo Olympic Games, Tokyo, Japan

MORE BIG AWARDS

BILES WAS NAMED THE AP FEMALE ATHLETE OF THE YEAR IN 2016 AND 2019!

Biles took some time away from training after the Rio Games. She focused on other projects.

Biles also used her time away from the gym to speak up about **abuse**. She became a powerful voice. She fought for other gymnasts and herself. She made gymnastics safer in the U.S.

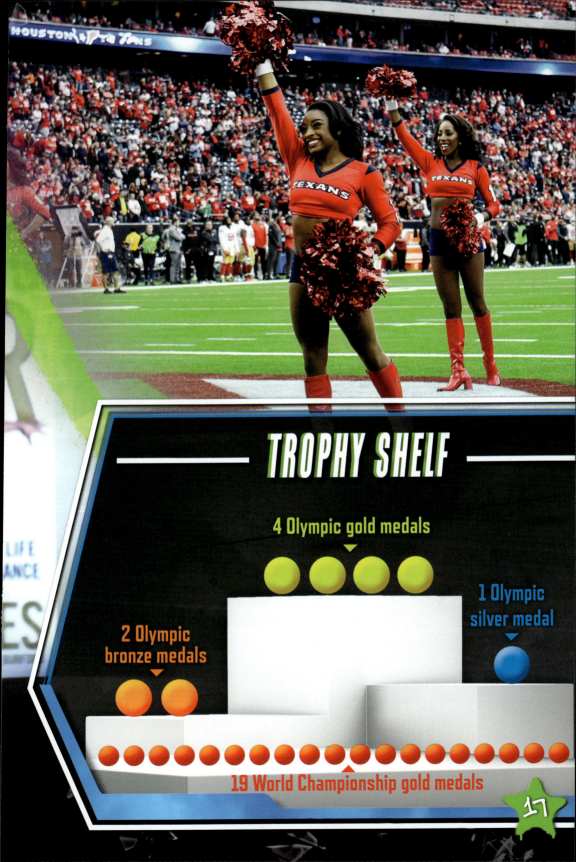

TROPHY SHELF

4 Olympic gold medals

1 Olympic silver medal

2 Olympic bronze medals

19 World Championship gold medals

17

Biles returned to competition in 2018. She won several more World Championship medals.

Biles took home two medals at the 2020 Tokyo Olympics. But she decided to pull out of many events. She needed to focus on her **mental health**. She showed the world it is okay to put herself first.

2020 TOKYO OLYMPICS
BRONZE MEDAL

TIMELINE

— 2003 —

Biles tries gymnastics for the first time at age 6

— 2013 —

Biles performs the Biles for the first time at the World Championships

BILES'S FUTURE

Simone Biles is one of the most successful gymnasts of all time. But she has not decided if she will push herself to win more. She may become a coach one day.

MEDAL OF FREEDOM

BILES WAS AWARDED THE PRESIDENTIAL MEDAL OF FREEDOM IN 2022. PRESIDENT JOSEPH BIDEN GAVE HER THE AWARD FOR MAKING POSITIVE CHANGE IN THE WORLD.

Biles continues to use her voice to help others. She often works to help children. Biles has shown the world that there is more to greatness than medals.

GLOSSARY

abuse—wrong or unfair treatment that is harmful

all-around—a category of gymnastics that includes all of the events; the all-around champion earns the highest total score from all events put together.

balance beam—a gymnastics event in which a gymnast performs moves on a long beam that is raised in the air

championships—contests to decide the best team or person

compete—to work for something for which another person is also working

floor exercise—a gymnastics event in which movements are performed on the floor in a special area

gymnastics—a sport in which competitors perform moves that show their balance and strength

junior—related to a competition between young people

mental health—the way people think and feel about themselves and the world around them

Olympic Games—worldwide summer or winter sports contests held in a different country every four years

vault—a gymnastics event in which a gymnast leaps over a form that was originally meant to mimic a horse

TO LEARN MORE

AT THE LIBRARY

Abdo, Kenny. *Simone Biles*. Minneapolis, Minn.: Abdo Zoom, 2021.

Adamson, Thomas K. *Olympic Records*. Minneapolis, Minn.: Bellwether Media, 2018.

Lawrence, Blythe. *The History of Gymnastics*. Minneapolis, Minn.: Abdo Publishing, 2021.

ON THE WEB

FACTSURFER

Factsurfer.com gives you a safe, fun way to find more information.

1. Go to www.factsurfer.com

2. Enter "Simone Biles" into the search box and click 🔍.

3. Select your book cover to see a list of related content.

INDEX

abuse, 16
all-around, 12
awards, 15, 20
balance beam, 14
Biles move, 4, 12, 13
childhood, 8, 9, 10
coach, 9, 20
family, 8
favorites, 11
floor exercise, 4, 10, 12, 14
future, 20
map, 15
Medal of Freedom, 20
medals, 4, 7, 10, 12, 13, 14, 17, 18, 21
mental health, 18

Olympic Games, 4, 7, 13, 14, 16, 18
profile, 7
Spring, Texas, 8
Team USA, 14
timeline, 18–19
trophy shelf, 17
U.S. Junior National Team, 10
USA Gymnastics National Championships, 12, 13
vault, 10, 14
World Championships, 7, 13, 18